Jan van Huysum's
Flower Piece

HENRIK WERGELAND

Translated from the Norwegian by
John Irons

Introduction by Ali Smith
Biographical Note by Tom Lotherington

MAIA

Published in 2008 by
The Maia Press Limited
82 Forest Road
London E8 3BH
www.maiapress.com

This edition is limited to 600 copies

Henrik Wergeland, *Jan van Huysums Blomsterstykke*
First published 1840; translation © 2008 John Irons
Introduction © 2008 Ali Smith
Biographical Note © 2008 Tom Lotherington

ISBN 978 1 904559 38 2

A CIP catalogue record for this book is available from
The British Library

Typeset in Poliphilus Roman and Van Dijck Italics
Flower ornaments created by Ole Larsen, used with permission

Printed and bound in Great Britain by Thanet Press
on paper from sustainable managed forests

Mixed Sources
Product group from well-managed
forests and other controlled sources
www.fsc.org Cert no. TT-COC-2023
© 1996 Forest Stewardship Council

The Maia Press is supported by Arts Council England

This edition is supported by

NORWEGIAN MINISTRY
OF FOREIGN AFFAIRS

NORLA

wergeland
20︵08

CONTENTS

Portrait of Henrik Wergeland (1808–45)
Lithograph by G. L. Fehr after a drawing
by J. Möller, Nasjonalbiblioteket, Oslo

INTRODUCTION

There is no poet in the world who's done what Henrik Wergeland can for an ordinary light-catching drop of common-or-garden water. In his poem, 'On The Sick Bed', dew has the power to wash the soul clean. In 'The Three', it's a kind of life-renewing baptismal. In 'Follow the Call', 'the poet's word' itself is a kind of dew. Poetry, purification, holy renewal, ordinariness; so far, so Romantic-commonplace. But it's specifically in his regard for the commonplace, in his understanding of the lit vitality of the 'common' and the life force of any very real 'garden', that Wergeland's poetic becomes remarkable, and this is most clearly visible, most joyfully played out, in one of his mature masterpieces, his 1840 *tour-de-force*, *Jan van Huysum's Flower Piece.*

Blake conceived of heaven in a wild flower; Wergeland takes a tiny fragment of fluid on a flower and gives it back to his readers as: a jewel, a pearl, a star, a parable, a piece of holiness, a piece of brevity, a piece of life itself held in the shape of a 'drop that can no more endure!' This eager, almost unbearable, perfectly held stasis is only the begin-ning; dew becomes a cosmos, a miracle, 'a wonder there's no telling.' 'Oh! the smallest drop is christ-ened / great.' More: casually, yet cornucopically, the dew image gathers power; it becomes a piece of sorrow in the shape of a teardrop, then a speck of water so fertile that not only can it feed new life into the ashes of gone life, it is also part of the process by which life ruined by history's worst foulness can be fully restored:

All is now as it once was:–
Covered by a heav'nly dew,
Earth returns it all anew.

Dew in this poem is a substance worth more than any royalty, more than any culmination of earthly riches. 'Your diamonds cannot make up for even one of the dewdrops on my flowers,' old Adrian tells the proud Dutch painter who throws all his wealth at the feet of the old man to try to buy the sublime bunch of flowers he has coaxed out of a heap of ashes, all that's left of his family.

But there's yet more to a tiny drop of water than this tumbling aggregation of images. Wergeland is very strikingly a poet in and of the real, fundamentally drawn to the life in art, and to what art actually does in the real world. Where Novalis suggested that ordinariness must be transfigured, Wergeland's preoccupation is with the aesthetic revelation of an already-there, simply-waiting-to-be-seen transfiguration in all things ordinary. At the opening of *Jan van Huysum's Flower Piece*, in his prologue of collected contemporary commentaries on van Huysum's paintings, every single one of the passages he selected passes comment on one particular skill which made the painter famous — the extraordinary lifelikeness of the dewdrops van Huysum painted on the flowers and fruits in his still-life work. You can almost feel Wergeland's delight at the commentators' recordings that viewers of paintings whose dewdrops look so real would lean forward to brush what they saw as real water off the painting. So, near the end of *Jan van Huysum's Flower Piece*, and after all the grandiose, gorgeous imaginings of dew as everything from teardrop to star, Wergeland simply imagines a very real, very wet drop of water falling 'out of the clear sky' on to the finished (real) Dutch painting whose imagined creation has been the subject of his poem. 'It bursts over the flowers. A marvel.' The final, very radical revelation of *Jan van Huysum's Flower Piece* is that regardless of riches, regardless of loss and renewal, regardless of interpretations, regardless of sorrows and happinesses and worlds lost and refound, the best thing dew can be is simply what it is, real beautiful dew.

Idiosyncratic, empathetic, near⁄rumbus⁄tious, Wergeland's poetic energy is a marvellous revelation. This is a poet, for instance, not just content to but keen to see the whole panorama of the world via the eyeball of his pet rabbit, as he does in one early poem – a poet who'd actually like to experience first⁄hand exactly how rabbits feel about grass. His poetic urge is a wide⁄open empathy, coupled with a belief that everything – grass, twigs, leaves – has its own voice, its own 'song'. 'He has no soul who won't believe / that Nature is an open book, / that moss's pallid rock⁄flowers have, / like roses, voice as well as look', as he writes in 'With a Bouquet'. To Wergeland, notions of nature are deeply connected to notions of word, book and soul. The interconnections he perceives between all things physical, aesthetic and metaphysical allow him to demonstrate that the small is conduit to the all, that the local is as universal as it gets, that if 'each life is but a mere leaf' then every leaf is momentous, sanctified.

But it's not Wergeland's forceful, radical openness of belief that strikes his modern reader so much as the contagious vigour of his work, in his voice, in his poetic eye. Wergeland's poetic pres⁄ence is like an enormous, bluntly persuasive word YES simply appearing on a reader's landscape; in the huge energy of his output he was determined above all, as he put it himself, to paint the real world, art, belief, and all the crucial animation of the connections between them, 'with a brush dipped in the sun'.

Henrik Wergeland is a poet almost unknown outside his native Norway, where he's held to be the pioneer of modern Norwegian literature and carries something of the same symbolic status as Burns does for Scotland. His poems are staple school texts, one of his works is broadcast every Christmas Eve on Norwegian radio and his figure looms large in any discussion of Norwegian national identity. This is partly because his figure did, in actuality, loom large in the very formation of Norwegian concepts of nationality – he was, literally, there at the birth of the nation.

He was born in 1808, the son of Nicolai Wergeland, a pastor and teacher and writer; this combination in his father allowed for a uniting of the powers of teaching, faith and literature in the son. He grew up in Eidsvoll, in a bedroom where 'birds flew about freely', as his sister Camilla wrote, a bedroom that's become legendary for its menagerie of live fish and grass snakes, its floor covered in moss and leaves and creatures. A combination of nature, politics and literature were, it seems, everyday family business to the Wergelands. Not only is Henrik one of the country's pioneering poetic figures but his sister wrote what would become the first modern Norwegian novel and his father was one of the original 112 men to draw up the first Norwegian Constitution in 1814, at the awarding of Norway to Sweden by the European powers (after Sweden lost Finland to Russia); Henrik Wergeland saw himself as an 'elder brother' to the Constitution itself.

There was nothing conventional about Wergeland as a public literary figure; the very notion of convention would have been enough to incite him to fisticuffs. He was a passionate public feuder (especially concerning the cause of Norwegian commonality versus Danish hierarchy), feted now for his didactic, headstrong, maddening combination of liability and likeability and for, on the one hand, his willingness to get so drunk that he'd pull all his clothes off and roll in the snow, and on the other his ability to be delicate enough to write a poem inviting a butterfly to come in through the window, land on his pen and bless his work with its own delicacy.

He was a republican who befriended kings and was close enough to King Karl Johan to be on a royal stipend for many years. He was paradoxical enough in his writings to have been claimed by political Norwegian Leftists and Rightists over the last century. He was a bankrupt, a flagrant sentimentaliser, a passionate educator, a fierce democrat – though a little slow, apparently, about including women in his calls for equality; his sister, however, can be credited with one of Norway's earliest feminist literary works in that first modern novel she wrote, *Amtmandens Døtre* (The County Governor's Daughters), and Wergeland's own *Flower Piece* was lovingly dedicated to one of Sweden's most outspoken feminist writers, his friend Fred, rika Bremer. A pragmatic Romantic, he worked for the enlightenment of the working-class Nor, wegian people, for cultural and official acceptance of the Norwegian language, and above all for the public education of all. 'You shall drive your plough with pride; you shall walk behind it as an enlightened free man, not as an empty-headed slave of darkness who knows nothing more than how to scatter oats in a furrow and then harrow them.'

If the tone of this is a little bullish, it's worth thinking of Wergeland as a tireless border, challenger – a gloriously paradoxical description for a figure so associated with definitions of national identity. Wergeland is most famed for his indefatigable call for national and religious open, ness and tolerance, particularly for his many years' long attempts to have Article 2 in the Norwegian Constitution, the article which denied Jews entry to the Kingdom of Norway, repealed. This was his political and poetic preoccupation in the decade before he died (and he died young, at 37, leaving 23 volumes of poems, pamphlets, essays, articles, stories, drama and fierce polemic behind him). When it came to religion it was a borderless family Wergeland imagined for the world. 'A great synod / Of all the parties / Has trampled down / Dogmas and ceremonies', as he wrote in 'Man'. Several of his late poems call for Norwegian presbyterianism to shift its position, to be open,

particularly to allow entry and assimilation for the
Jews. In a poem called 'The Maple and the Pine'
he gives a closed proud country an ultimatum – to
choose between dry fixedness and the sheer joy and
sweetness that comes of openness; in 'The Three'
he imagines, like a coming together of three
different birds on a branch into one dawn song
made of three different birdsongs, a coming
together of Christian, Muslim and Jew in an easy,
respectful, dawn praising of the same God, a
nameless God shared by an 'unfettered' people.

Wergeland is a tireless passer-on of imagina-
tive positive vision. 'There is nothing, great or
small, / that is fruitless, or decayed / but its ending
keeps a purpose.' A poet besotted by expression
and fiercely opposed to repression; a poet who
could grace everything he touched in Norwegian,
or what he called 'the bands of a minor tongue',
with the major force of his positivity; a manipu-
lator, in equal part, of sentiment, comedy and
visionary originality; a poet who was always polit-
ical, and a politicker who could hear the voices of
flowers; his output was always written fast and
loose. Its vividness of image – for instance in
'Christmas Eve', which closes with its old Nor-
wegian couple in front of their fire on Christmas
morning, struggling to straighten out the frozen
arms and legs of two corpses, those of their child
and of an old Jewish traveller whom they'd refused
shelter the freezing, stormy night before, only to
find that the man was trying to return them their
own daughter – neutralises any damaging senti-

mentality and reveals a symbiosis of light and dark⁄ness at the centre of his poetic.

Even on his death⁄bed he was optimistic; death itself is a central part of the good life of all things, he suggested repeatedly in his last, best works. It's a gifted, open, borderless kind of person who can vacate his or her own life–death melo⁄drama; when he was dying, Wergeland enjoyed imagining the sheer beauty of the flowers living well after his own demise.

This is typical of his aesthetic openness and of the generosity of his art. 'Let it suffice that all around is good'.

Jan van Huysum's Flower Piece is a fable⁄poem which imaginatively explores the source, not just of a single piece of art but of the notion of art itself. It begins, after a critical round⁄up of pieces about the Dutch painter van Huysum, with a discussion of the all⁄too⁄human problems of clumsiness, over⁄enthusiasm, blundering critical faculty. It covers the foul powerplay of history, the consequence of religious intolerance, the force of human grief and loss, the reblossoming of human hope, the connection between platonic ideal concepts and realities, the good workings of art, the demands of art on the artist, the demands of the artist on life, and the ways in which art, life, immortality and the divine interconnect. It ends announcing its own slightness – nothing but a tale told by a painted rosebud. Then it reminds its readers of the hardwon miracle that a mere flower, or a work of art (a flower with a voice, as it were), actually is. It reminds us that nothing is unconnected, that 'the rose-bud is your kin'.

It does all this in an interplay between the poet's interjections about art and poetry and the arresting fable of a holy man, Adrian, whose wife, children and household are burnt to death before his eyes in a religious war. Adrian subsequently coaxes a bouquet of flowers quite literally out of their ashes, and the bouquet, in turn, quite literally restores his family to him whole. It is a cultivation which blends, in a stunning piece of poetic imag-ining, the pain of the loss and the happiness of the love into the same experience, the same human sensation.

But the flowers are so beautiful that Jan van Huysum, who just happens to be passing, cuts them down and takes them. The cutting of the flowers is as painful to Adrian as the original death of the family; the painter inherits a great deal of suffering for his selfish actions. The final painting is a proof not just of the fineness of immortality but also the rough road between immortality and mortality. Meanwhile the poem, about a painting, about the representation of 'flower-cadavers that yet live', acts as a chain of connection between utterly different-seeming things: mortality and immortality, art and war, life and art, pain and happiness, death and rebirth. Art begets mercy begets life begets understanding begets art begets loss begets life.

Wergeland is rewriting the Book of Job here; certainly the figure of Job is behind the poem's tenet against self-indulgence, its extraordinary vision of Adrian's restored happiness. But what kind of poet is it who can give innocence back, as Wergeland does here, to centuries of historical holocaust? In the shape of a lyric poem *Jan van Huysum's Flower Piece* is a huge act of kindness, an act of restoration, and an anatomising of how both aesthetic and natural restoration function; a poem almost insolent in its 'joyous, guiltless making', it breaks into galloping prose rather like an action-packed film, because Wergeland knows exactly how to spin the right kind of gripping yarn, how to go for the jugular, how to entertain an audience, and at the same time sustain such opposite notions of sanctity in reality, of mercy in war, of humaneness in bombast, and how to frame a moment of understanding that will melt fixity of belief and allow a new fluidity of understanding.

The poem is a feat of holy-fool energy fired up by steady intellectual optimism. It knows what it means to perish, and it does not sell this knowledge short. Then it remakes the perished, perishable world in leaves and flowers as surely as spring itself does – and as surely as an Old Master can. It holds itself, like the dewdrop, 'shattering and yet still whole', in disparate, almost irreconcilable pieces which fuse, like its handling of pasts and futures, into a single work, a single moment, a single, fused, aesthetic and real, experience of alive⁄ness. It suggests that real life blood runs between nature, life, art and all faiths open to mercy and renewal.

'Only one angel has stayed faithful to man: the wingless, indifferent ones, with dead eyes, fat cheeks and complacent smile, like all angels except Raphael's, are painted in the churches. He will lead you past suffering with averted eyes' ('The Thistledown Gatherer'). It is time Wergeland — the poet of dew, the transcriber of the voices of flowers, the demander of liberty, the rumbunctious and outrageous optimist, the wishful⁄thinking visionary, the responsible bard, the politicker, the lover of commonality, the paradox of feuding opposites — took his place internationally alongside his true kin, writers such as Byron, Rousseau, Novalis, Coleridge, Blake, Hugo, Pushkin, Burns. A hundred years after his death, Walter Benjamin conjured an angel of history, the bladed wings of which Wergeland would have appreciated; a hundred and fifty years after Wergeland died, Italo Calvino might have been thinking about just such a writer when he suggested, in his *Six Memos for the Next Millennium*, that a crucial impetus for the writing of anything is the hearing and giving of voices to all those people – and things – whose voices go unheard.

Right now, as religious arguments polarise the world once more, Wergeland's own voice seems pretty timeless. His symbolic seminality, and the act of generosity at the core of his art – and of all real art – couldn't be more relevant.

ALI SMITH, 2008

Opposite: title page of first edition
Nasjonalbiblioteket, Oslo

Jan van Huysums

Blomsterstykke.

En Buket

fra

Henr. Wergeland til Fredrika Bremer.

„Anch'io sono pittore."
Corregio.

Kristiania.

**Trykt i Guldberg & Dzwonkowskis Officin
ved C. Risum.**

—

1840.

Jan van Huysum's
Flower Piece

A BOUQUET

FROM HENR. WERGELAND
TO FREDRIKA BREMER

'Anch'io sono pittore' Correggio

Translated by John Irons

JOHAN (JAN) VAN HUYSUM
(BORN AMSTERDAM 1682 – DIED 1749)

'Is father Justus, a mediocre painter, was the first to instruct him, although he subsequently learned from Nature, who offered him her most beautiful daughters as models. He is the Raphael of the floral kingdom; its inhabitants he portrayed with inimitable fidelity. His flowers are resplendent in the loveliest colours and with a natural freshness, as if the dew had just poured its pearls over them. In his flower pieces he also introduced insects, butterflies, birds, their nests with eggs, etc. – with everything in Nature's rich and magnificent apparel. He often placed his flowers in vases, adorned with beautiful bas-reliefs. The execution of his works bears witness to the utmost diligence, and in preparing his colours, oil and varnish he studiously avoided the gaze of strangers and observed the deepest secrecy. He glazed endlessly, even the body colours, making use in doing so of the clearest and most enduring colours – ones that have also retained their freshness even to the present day. The flowers that have been painted on a clear or brownish ground are generally preferred to those on a dark one – and these are particularly expensive. A mental illness he suffered during his later years had no detrimental influence on his art.'

(*Naglers Künstler-Lexicon*)

— 'The 18th century's most excellent painter of flowers and fruits felt a particular inclination to depict species of the vegetable kingdom, focusing the entire power of his painter's brush on exhausting all his art in the truetolife imitation of them. He gained perfection in his flower and fruit pieces. He knew how to spy out Nature's secrets, to capture the fleeting moment of flowering at its most beautiful and to reach perfection in this genre through the captivating truth and diversity of his colours and the almost transparent quality of his fine floral creations. He was the first artist to portray flowers on a clear ground, surpassing all his predecessors in softness and freshness, in the delicacy and life of his colours, in the expression of the lushness of the plants and the minutest portrayal of the conditions of light. He was so jealous of his art that he did not allow anyone to watch him at work.

His flowers are more beautiful and true than his fruits – the dewdrops and insects he added possess the highest degree of lifelikeness. For each of his paintings he charged 1,000–1,400 guilders; two of his watercolours . . . have in recent times fetched 10,000 guilders in the Netherlands.'

(*Allg. deutsche Real-Encyklopädie*)

— 'He surpassed all his predecessors in painting flowers and fruits, and his work gained such a reputation that only monarchs and the richest of private persons were able to purchase his paintings. The finest taste, the most brilliant colouring, the most forceful brush and perfect imitation of Nature give works by this artist an immense value. In his landscape paintings he can stand comparison with the great masters, but when it comes to painting flowers and fruits, he is absolutely unrivalled. The lustreless, fur-like quality of the fruits, the glistening quality of the flowers, the transparency of the dewdrops, the lively sense of movement he knew how to impart to his insects – everything in his paintings is sheer rapture.'

(*Allgemeines Künstlerlexicon, cf. Pierers Encyklopäd. Wörterbuch*)

— 'Solely by virtue of his genius he gained the highest rank in his art. In his flowers he has represented their entire truth, their most brilliant colours with so gentle and pleasant a brush that Nature herself is no truer. His fruits have a trans-

parency – especially his grapes – that allow one to
see the cellular tissue and the juice with which they
are filled. One almost believes that the insects
move. And his dewdrops? The first time one sees
them, one is tempted to wipe them off, lest they
spoil the masterpiece.'

(*Marquis d'Argens, Examen critique*)

— 'He has, so to speak, competed with
Nature. Freshness, charm, elegance, truth,
colouring. He would be the god of spring, if Flora
had also given him her fragrance.'

(*Galerie du Musée Napoléon*)

— 'Achieved in his painting of flowers and
fruits a perfection that surpassed everything previ-
ously seen within this genre. All the florists with
whom he was acquainted competed with each
other in informing him about the most beautiful
produce of their gardens. He used to work out
simple studies on his own, using them as a basis for
composing his paintings and was, it is said, so
singular that he never allowed anyone access when
at his work, making a great secret of the prepara-
tion of his oils, varnishes and colours. Even his
own brother was not permitted to watch him at
work, and it was only with great difficulty that he
was persuaded to instruct *Margaretha Havermann*,
of whose talents he is said to have been jealous.
Vexation at the behaviour of one of his sons so
affected his mind that he fell into a kind of
madness which, nevertheless, did not influence his

art in any way. As to his style, he executed every-
thing with good sense and incredible diligence,
glazing again and again, even the body colours.
This is the reason why his fruits are too beautiful,
or, to be more precise, they end up resembling fruits
made of wax or coloured ivory; but his flowers, his
insects, the dew and the individual dewdrops
surpass everything previously seen of this kind.
Information about his most excellent works is
provided by both Gool and Descamps.

(*Fiorillo, Geschichte der zeichnenden Künste*)

— 'Lovers of especially magnificent finish
place v.H. above all flower painters. The diligence
with which he chose the most resplendent and solid
colours, prepared them and cleansed the oil greatly
contribute to the brilliant freshness of his works.
The white grounding of his boards or canvases,
Descamps states, was prepared with the greatest
care and with a purity that freed him from the fear
of seeing the colours, which he applied with great
spontaneity, become torn or spoiled. Everything is
handled with precision, without any sign of negli-
gence, but also without dryness. The rough, the
smooth, the velvety, the transparent, the truest and
most brilliant brightness – all of this is found here
with that flourish that Nature indicates, and that
cannot be ascribed either to manner or chance. His
vases, which he knew how to position effectively,
and in which he placed his flowers, are also true to
Nature. The bas reliefs, just as fine as everything
else, are well-composed and of studied harmony.

He had the good taste to form his groups in such a way that the brightest flowers took centre-stage, and he made use of the colour specific to each individual flower in order to gradually tone down the colours from the central point to the outermost edge of the group. Bird's nests, their eggs, the feathers, the insects, the butterflies, the dewdrops – everything is portrayed with the greatest veracity and produces the most perfect illusion.'
(*Heidenreichs aesthetisches Wörterbuch*)

Lüdemanns Geschichte der Mahlerei and *Hirts Kunstbemerkungen* concur with the above judgements.

In 'Historische Erklärungen der Gemälde, welche *Herr Gottfried Winkler* in Leipzig gesammelt, Leipz. 1768' the very piece by v. Huysum that is the subject of the present poem is described thus:
'Diverse flowers have been collected in a vessel decorated with raised figures and placed in a niche. The queen of flowers is resplendent on the sisterly side of the light Guelderland rose, surrounded by beautifully striped tulips, flowering poppy and white narcissi, whose splendour gaily coloured auriculae, double hyacinths, etc. as well as a host of spring's tender creatures heighten with their gentler grace. Multicoloured butterflies and various insects are drinking the morning dew from their petals, which the attentive gaze seems to penetrate and Zephyr's gentle breath seems playfully to rustle. Below on the wall, the domestic snail

clings fast and to the right there is a bird's nest with three abandoned eggs. The painting is on wood, is 2ft 9½in high and 2ft 2in wide. Its former owner was *Mr. Dietrich Schmid* in Amsterdam, to whom the master gave it as a memento of friendship.' For a number of years, it has since been in the posses⁄ sion of Prefect *Thygeson*. There it made an impres⁄ sion of the author which he has here sought to impart. It comprises, in a somewhat more detailed although not exhaustive description than above, in a vase a white⁄variegated tulip, and a dark, red⁄brown one of genuine Dutch magnificence, a white rose, two red roses, a seringa, a brown auricula, daffodils (narcissi), a fiery poppy, a yellow, double marigold, a double red⁄variegated carnation, a blue hyacinth, a convolvulus, a forget⁄ me⁄not, a half⁄open rosebud and a delphinium. In addition, a bird's nest with eggs, a snail complete with shell, a couple of flying insects and some dewdrops that the observer will more than once have had the inclination to dab dry.

These are the elements of this admirable composition, which cannot be made more wonderful by mine, which, although it has been inspired by the rapturous moment of contempla⁄ tion, is still too poor not to call for some indulgence to dare call itself a bouquet to the brilliantly gifted paintress who has chosen for her exquisite paint⁄ brush the even finer flowers of the human heart and of life than those of *van Huysum*.

THE CONTEMPLATION

Clumsy human admiration
that needs air and lips to say it!
Clumsier than the shy wonder
humble beasts display, you blunder
wholly in your adoration
squander in rapt adulation; —
with your passion's savage heart
you misuse your love and slay it:
your adored unsullied art.

     Woe, if now that I need utter
(so compelled I sense my breast
gently moan when it is pressed)
I should cause this drop to flutter
from *van Huysum*'s soft rose petal
shaken by my lips' rough breath!

Spring breeze, giddy, slow to settle,
shows more mercy if you will:
Dew's bright gleam from grove and hedge
rain with iridescent edge,
hid in lady's-mantle folds
every drop the eye beholds
it has plundered recklessly
in the air has scattered free
. . . *this one* only lies there still,
at its rim like teardrop borne
trembling by an eyelash worn,
outmost in your diadem,
anguish that is sweet and tender
rolled on by your weighty gem;
lovely as the pearl whose splendour
merits it the heart of stars;
full as Magdalena's tears
full and heavy, almost bursting;
shattering and yet still whole,
as sound counsel ripeness nears
in an angel's saddened soul.
      Oh! the smallest drop is christened
great which on that petal glistened.
Glistened? Yes, has it not vanished,
like a word's for ever banished
once the mouth did it impart
from the still ground of its heart?
Every instant seemed to call
for its weight to cause it fall.
      That it should be ever spilling
ever with more gleam be swelling,
ever trickling and yet filling,

— is a wonder there's no telling,
at which I amazed do ponder
art's great virtue, Nature's error,
as if sound were captured there,
speeding swallow in the air,
image in the spring's clear mirror.
     Oh, what dread with sweet allure!
Fear of wind and sun's bright ray
Drop that no more can endure!
Fly that wants to speed away!
     Snail that now its house would move
to the leaf below, above!
Painted leaf that up would strive!
Flower-cadavers that yet live!
Oh, what dread with sweet allures!
While I stare at their profusion
I encounter in confusion
features of long-past amours.
Oh, although you are so true
I can scarce believe you grew
'mongst the others on our earth
but in Eden had your birth:
Flowers! that you are therefore
flowers for certain and yet more:
Flowers of flowers, these corpses all
that enthral us in the garden
as pure spirits in God's heaven
are like corpses in their pall.
     Ah, like this bouquet in fashion
would most likely love appear
with its swarm of burning passion
as if lover, while embracing

with abandon his most dear,
had his heart cleft at the seams,
so one in a flash of sight
(swiftly as a glimpse one spies
of a phantom taking flight)
could discern its inmost dreams,
its unspoken aspirations
its unborn deliberations
its sworn oath before it dies
in a faithless breath of air –
while it still is lying there
as a new-born, pure and fair,
who'll turn into an offender –
its full hope, ere wings sprout tender
like the flower's heart-leaf tips,
its first words ere they are spoken
its great joy ere it has broken
and a smile has touched its lips.

     Where is found so great a passion,
such great pleasure, choked by pain,
such a muffled heartbeat's hush,
such a glow on lips that kiss,
such a bleeding heart-wound's stain
as in that tulip's deep abyss,
in the dark nocturnal scarlet
of this self-consuming garnet,
this convulsive, sickly flush!

     How delightful is the bliss,
the intoxicating instant
of love's sweetness when her yes
she gave to you, seen in the two
red roses that each other meet!

After kisses, such a thirst
that they both burn with fierce heat?
How must love's remorse now hurt,
blushing red with paleness strive
in this whiteness so serene?
Where an urge for joy so thrive
as in this carnation's sheen?
Where a blood that so can glimmer
as its garnet dew⁄rain's shimmer
scattered o'er the pearl's frail skin?
Sweet devotion's keenest eyes
never saw in distant skies
for Zion's blessèd sons a frieze
of such festive great marquees
as convolvuli here spread
bluer than the heaven's bed,
finer than the modest veil
placed before the bridal mouth.
Innocence can boast no blue
so fine nor cold so shorn
as the hyacinth adorn;
tenderness so fine in muster
as the lilac's full deployment:
every small flower in its cluster
is its own small vase, with lustre
of a porcelain's half⁄shine,
full of honey's sweet enjoyment
full of butterflies' rich wine.

Are so pure an angel's mind,
virgin's thoughts, a new⁄born's dream
and the martyr's tearful stream
as Narcissus' pallid star!

Oh, therein the saint will find
his devotions mirrored are;
for, despite its stem so raised,
it has bowed its pious head,
as if God in prayer it praised,
as if innocence could err
as if it had sinned instead.
And where could a thought be bred
in a young man's brilliant brain
fiery as on flaming cheek
of this blood-red poppy sleek?
And where such an ardent plan
in manhood's heart is ever thought
as the flaming vault whose span
in this tulip stretches taut?
And where did there sigh a prayer
that was e'er so chaste and fair
as that slender blue-eyed Mary
which so humbly, coyly clings
– coy as thought of silent tears –
to a moss-rose bud so clear?
And where is the bard that sings
equal to this mute small thing
Floral mysteries, the chary,
if but once it bared its art
and its rosy lips would part?
      Oh, could this bud speak to me,
and a spirit it inspire
Oh, I'd beg it if I could
(beauties may be begged with fire)
to inform me if it would
how such flowers came to be!

THE DUTCH FAMILY

'*Alonzo de Tobar*! Where are you, Alonzo? Alonzo! Brave Castilian! are you not following the colonel? Adelante, Caballero! adelante!'

Alonzo de Tobar, the unhappy painter who had become an enlisted soldier of the conqueror of his fatherland, Louis XIV, because he could never be a *Velazquez* or the pride of Spain, *Bartolomeo Esteban Murillo*, has remained behind. 'Forward Walloons! Forward! The colonel has given you the village. Viva el coronel! He cares no more for Dutch villages than Alba and Luxembourg, the friend of the Devil.'

Alonzo de Tobar has remained behind. He who his wild companions called the Wolf of the Sierra and who has never remained behind during the destruction of a heretical town, has turned his horse and bows his head in tears over its mane.

Does he still despair at the great Murillo's 'Santa Katharina's Betrothal' or at Velazquez's 'Family'? Ha! There the last of the cuirassiers come rushing past, shouting 'Great Alonzo de Tobar! Little Murillo! Brave Castilian! are you not following the colonel? Adelante, Caballero! adelante!'

He has heard his mother moaning under the hoofbeats, or seen the Madonna in the cloud of smoke that belches full of sparks, now black as night, then white as a cloud, enormous as a moun-tain, out over the church. The Madonna otherwise inspired him to destroy the heretics, and the fanatic Spaniard destroyed so as to be inspired to become a Murillo and to be able to paint 'Santa Katharina's Betrothal'.

For when he stood in front of it in the Cathe-dral of Seville, the city of Murillo's birth, he fell to the ground in recognition of the fact that he was no Murillo. And then he sought out the French standard among the wildest of its warriors, the Walloons. He believed he could fire his artistic inspiration and powers by nurturing the fervour of fanaticism in a horrific war against heretics. He was waging war on them, while he had been enlisted to wage war on those in political power, the enemies of his master.

Oh, how deathly pale the lead spire of the church looks against the smoke soaring up behind it, dark, dense, motionless like a mountain, or against the spire of flame that shoots up from the chancel, ever higher, more magnificent and auda/ cious? Alas! there are cries from within – the church must be full of women and children.

The Walloons fight with each other at the door for the spoils that lie inside. The vicar's daughter, *Katharina*, had just got married when they broke into the village and she had been left behind in the confusion – she and her bridesmaids. 'Alonzo de Tobar, don't you want to join in?' a fellow/countryman shouts, as, on the shoulders of the others, he hauls himself up into the chancel window and looks down at the flaming church, full of women. 'Ah, Paraiso de Demonio! Ah, le paradis de l'enfer! Oh, paradise of hell! And Alonzo, you hang back?'

Alonzo hangs back, bowed over his steed. He will be expelled by the Luxembourg fils perdus, he will lose the name of Wolf, he will be hanged for his softness. But the hot/blooded, fanat/ ical Castilian would rather die with dishonour than be part of the destruction of *this* village.

Woe to his consumed soul! So many Dutch villages has he torched, rejoicing among his comrades 'en la honra de nuestra Sennora!' but this village, this one was too lovely, the cottages too tidy, the church too venerable like a priest among them, the flower gardens in front of them too beautiful. Ivy and climbing roses had entwined the gables; hollyhocks stood on guard outside the doors.

A frightful cry tells that the church now belongs to the Walloons and the flames. With increased force it bursts out of the broken-open door and the smashed chancel window from where Katharina's bridegroom, his bride under one arm, has thrown down Alonzo's fellow countryman. He comes into view there at the same instant as the Walloons swarm in through the door.

Thanks be to the forces of desperation and sure-footedness! thanks be to the arm of the old ivy! It bore the bride down at her lover's breast. Alonzo has seen her in the window and when from the place of horror she hastens to the house of her father, the vicar, the house next to the church, the most venerable of them all, with the lightest, friendliest windows, with the most charming flower garden outside, with the densest ivy over the roof, from which the flames are already shooting.

Alonzo de Tobar, the painter, has seen the wonder of the village, the province, the Netherlands. 'Katharina,' he murmurs — and the bowed-down figure of the cavalryman comes to life – 'I have seen Katharina, *my* Katharina, not that of Murillo and yet as beautiful. Ha, that was Murillo's Katharina transfigured! Her dark eyes have become seraphic blue, her appearance more transparent, her colour of a more star-like white-ness; countenance, expression even more spiritu-alised. Ha, Alonzo de Tobar's 'Katharina' shall surpass that of Murillo, just as an angel surpasses the most magnificent human being!'

Alonzo has leapt from his horse. He follows the maiden, who, with outstretched arms as if crucified, rushes towards her father's door. 'O milagro de Dios!' A grey-haired man who, with jubilation in his eyes, while his features could not as quickly let go of their horror, opened the door for those in flight, taking the girl into his arms, and shouted: 'Katharina! Oh, God be praised!'

'She is a Katharina, and a bride. The wedding wreath fluttered from her locks. O milagro de Dios! It is a sign from heaven!'

The Spaniard has stopped at the door. He can hear hymn singing inside, and amongst the voices one that is like that of a divine harp. 'Heaven is merciful; Alonzo de Tobar is also to be the pride of Spain, the painter king of Castile, just as the great Murillo is that of Andalusia and Seville. I have seen the sister-soul of Murillo's Katharina. God has seen Murillo's Katharina and created a second one in her image for Alonzo de Tobar.

Alonzo rushes towards the door in a rage.

'Ayuden los angelos! Are you mad, do you not wish to be saved? The roof is on fire, the tower is reeling, the flames are driving the Walloons before them out of the church and this way, this way! They are more terrible than the flames.'

Inside, the vicar was kneeling, the venerable *Adrian*, with a bible raised in his trembling hands; at his side his faithful *Margaretha* and around them first the pride of the family, the bride *Katharina*, who has swiftly found her place: with one arm round her mother's neck, the other round that of her bridegroom, *Johan*, the dashing young man; then the pious, nun-like *Narcissa*, with a fine streak of red on her deathly pale cheeks, she whose lover had fallen in the heroic battle of Leiden; then *Hyacinth*, the handsome, blue-eyed boy, and his sister, the slim, delicate *Elisabeth*; little *Benjamin* and his twin sister *Anna*, 'little Anna', with their heads in their mother's lap and covered by their nurse, faithful old *Magdalena*: and farthest off, almost outside the circle, the eldest daughter *Klara*, whose tragic passion for an enemy soldier – perhaps the slayer of Narcissa's betrothed – had suffused her face with a pallor that, even so, less commanded the sympathy of the family than one might have believed of these so gentle and good people.

'Ayuden los santos! They're coming!' Alonzo shouts outside. 'Away with you! The house belongs to me.' A single sabre can be heard against

many. 'They're coming!' Johan shouts, hurrying
towards the door. 'On your knees!' the old man
commands. 'Only God can save.' And the circle
closes in more tightly. 'Save us! The Walloons . . .'
Narcissa shrieks, her hands in front of her eyes.
'We will be saved!' shouts Klara with a tinge of a
flush on her cheeks; for she seemed to have heard
the Spaniard's voice. 'Yes, we will be saved' – the
father moans, wringing his hands – 'May God
have mercy on us! Come, Klara, my child! Every-
thing is forgiven. God be praised! Now we will be
saved. For the flames will reach us before the
terrible – '

The flames surge over in huge waves, beams
from the burning church fall over the house, shake
it to its very foundations, and the fire makes open-
ings where they can attack.

'In here! In here, comrades! La doncella
aqui!' Alonzo's fellow countryman, who rejoiced
in the paradise of hell when he looked down into
the church full of women, has broken open the
door. 'Abajo los hereticos!' The Walloons rush in;
the flames from the other side. Alonzo has not
been able to stop them. 'It's him!' cries Klara,
embracing his legs. He pushes her away cruelly as
once before, and, fighting against his wild fellow
countryman, tries to seize Katharina, who is pulled
away by her father and her bridegroom to the other
side, towards the flames. At the same instant —
— At the same instant . . .

God! Heavens! What has happened?

The church tower has crashed on to the house, through its roof already virtually consumed by the flames. Everything is buried beneath: Alonzo's fellow countryman, who from raging desire had leapt into the middle of the circle of those kneeling, Katharina and her bridegroom, the mother, Klara and the other children, and the servant – everyone except the father and Alonzo, who, on their separate sides, were furthest away from the spot where the collapse took place. But Katharina was no longer among them. Alas, neither of them has Katharina!

It was a frightful instant, and yet the previous one, when the wild warriors appeared at the door, had been even more terrible.

The two who had been saved had been flung far off. Fortune is the caprice of misfortune. Adrian wakes up. It was night. The Walloons had done their work: nothing left of the town. Only the smoke held down by the cold of the night lay like a blue-white lake above the plots of land. A dark figure bends down over the old man. He recognises the Spaniard by his helmet plume, and with a shudder pulls the tabard that the latter out of pity has spread over him over his head. The stars gazed calmly down as if nothing had happened, and the frogs sang in the canal that slowly wound its way through the plain. Only the storks seemed to be in mourning, for they stood in a flock down by the water's edge, the heads tucked under their wings.

Their nests too had been burned.

It would be dawn in an hour. The storks
have already flown away when the Spaniard shakes
Adrian awake from a sleep that resembles death so
much that it did not even breathe. 'Was she your
daughter, old man?' Alonzo asks with a hollow
voice.

'Who?'
'Her, old man! la querida del cielo! You saw
it, and must understand me.'
'I had five: Klara and Katharina and . . .'
'Katharina; I mean no other. O mea caritta!'
The old man laughs up into his eyes.
'Madonna! He is mad. Old man, old man,
collect your thoughts.'
Adrian laughs even more violently. The
warrior shudders.
'If it was not her, if you were not her father
but only the heretical vicar who was to desecrate
her head with your blessing, I would fling you into
the glowing embers – and it would be an act of
mercy.'
The madman stares at him, and cowers.
Woe is me! Alonzo murmurs. 'I have lost
my ideal, which was to have let Alonzo de Tobar
surpass Esteban Murillo. But does a divine revela-
tion last longer? I will hurry back to Spain, and in
a monastery pray heaven to recall her image in my
memory.'
The old man continues to stare long after the

warrior has left – the man who is frenziedly rushing over the plain and who would be hanged, along with all his ambitious painter's plans, were he to run into the squadron, that dark line moving over there under the horizon, like the shadow of a cloud.

Ha, there they discover him. The squadron fans out. The hunt begins for a laggard and deserter. But the faithful, wise horse that sought and found its master, takes the reins so as also to save him; and thus *Alonzo Michael Tobar* escapes, he who was to become the most successful imitator of the great Bartolomeo Esteban Murillo. But the work that earns him a place among Spain's artists is a 'Santa Katharina's Betrothal', in which he is most original and which vies with Murillo's painting for the palm of victory, as well as 'Family', which almost rivals Velazquez's masterpiece. It has at least all the gentle faces of Adrian's family.

But who knows anything of Alonzo de Tobar? Who knows even Spain's greatness, Spain's brilliant greatness, which it possesses because it has managed to preserve its national individuality? The world knows only the greatness of its misfortunes.

OLD ADRIAN'S FLOWERBED

Years have passed by. A cottage stands
where once the vicarage stood. Solitary it stands
there, without any neighbours. Itinerant members
of the few in the congregation who were able to flee
have built it for their former vicar, whom they
found among the ruins.

It is a beautiful day in spring. The sun also
shone cordially and piously that day when the
Walloons destroyed the village. Old Adrian is
busy outside the cottage, sowing and planting in
the ash-mingled earth. He knows this is the spot,
for he has found his Margaretha's engagement ring
there and a sprig of her lilac outside the window,
under which she used to sit with her children. He

has brought new life to it; and now he is sowing and planting round it, murmuring: 'God will give his blessing, God will give his blessing.' Strangers often went past, laughed and asked: 'how many people haven't had their houses burnt to the ground without going mad?'

But who would ever imagine that the old gardener digging so eagerly and yet so measuredly, taking so much care to water and cover his plants, busying himself so nimbly in his flowerbed, was insane? – His hair was probably whiter, but smooth and shiny as before, his cheeks redder, his eyes clearer and more fiery. And he could smile to himself when he discovered a shoot, yet another leaf on his dear plants. Then he would murmur: 'God will give his blessing!' and bend down, make the sign of the cross and whisper the divine blessing over them.

Some time passed. The lilac grew. Every-thing blossomed around it. *Holland*, Flora's favourite floor, had never borne such miracles of perfection and beauty. It was a summer evening, after a mild shower. A few drops lay heavy and full once more on the leaves. With quivering lips the old man sat over his flowering treasure.

— 'Oh my soul, be strong, don't shirk!
Bear the Almighty's wondrous work!
Still, my breast, cease every heave,
so my spirit may perceive,

and thought not be led astray
by a heart that beats away!
Spare my hearing, though you call me,
though you charm and you enthral me,
music of sweet ecstasy
that is surging in my ears!
Do not blind my gaze, sweet tears!
Though I weep, may I yet see
as with thousand eyes clear gazing,
as the stars in blazing shield,
that great miracle amazing
which to us has been revealed!

    Woe that madness, woe to me
poor wretch, blinder than the blind
should God's wonder I dispute!
Does the sun when most intense,
at the zenith of its route
shine as *this* on sight and sense?
Must a brow dashed on a rock
to its cost its hardness mock?
Does a mother truly feel
from her all too painful bliss
life born of her pledge of love?
Or the lover that but she,
sighed and longed for, is who he
tightly clasps in burning kiss?

    Mercy, heart so mild a treasure
in spirit of the Trinity,
greater wonders does command
with omnipotent left hand
than e'en dreaming angels see,
while his wisdom – for to measure

ocean depths and distance far,
regulate each wayward star
strictly by the sun's strong rays,
tether every shooting comet,
govern so that all obeys,
and the humblest worm perceives it –
only his right hand displays.
    Oh, who tried the Almighty's powers?
Oh, who sought wisdom's peak to find,
glimpse the light which, fed on gloom
of suns and on mulch of stars,
does all angels render blind,
and which does all thought consume?
    Man can hide within his breast
his own heart at his behest, —
Who the heart of God has e'er perceived?
Who the womb of pure compassion
where the wonder was conceived
born now in amazing fashion?
Is not born in hidden bower
Son of sin and child of earth?
Oh who dares view in that hour
Mercy in her pangs of birth,
when, pregnant with the Almighty's power,
God's love conceives the miracle
it now lets happen on this earth?
    I have seen it! Oh *Margrethe,*
Never were there wonders greater!
God be praised for sense and mind!
God be praised I am not blind
as my former, wild lament,
which was blinder than all stone,

bluffer than Job's in intent.
All once more to me's been sent,
As before is everything,
All again as leaves in spring,
no one's missing, no not one.
      In these flowers has God anew
Given life to all of you.
Your souls' blood has now been poured
in their roots by the great Lord,
so I every feature see
in the flower so known to me,
hear beloved hearts that beat,
feel their pulse, their thoughts can read,
see the rays of well-known eyes
in the flower bowls that I prize
just as clear as I once knew.
Yea, what wonders God can do!
Time's wreath that was broken quite
he once more has bound aright:
as a child's nurse tales of yore
to my senses roused once more
gently whispers at my ear.
Oh, what sweet sounds do I hear!
Margarethe's voice once more
blithely laughing as before
by the rustled lilac bush;
the flower's wondrous violet flush,
blue and red both bathed in white,
dim as yet behind the leaves —
oh, and dare I lift aside?
dare I risk this wondrous sight? —
nothing other have I spied

than the shade of her own veil,
that she wore when, each day sitting
with her head devout and pale
over stitches and her knitting,
daily tasks she'd interweave.
    I'd be more than blind, had not
I my *little Anna's* eye
recognised as being nigh
here in this forget‑me‑not.
    Oh, the more on it I gaze
do I see my child's own face,
from all others set apart.
God, my child, bless you, dear heart,
Round your own twin‑brother's waist
your arms now as always rest:
And the rose‑bud is your kin,
Little Anna and *Benjamin* . . .
Over both there petals rest
with pure droplets silver‑laden
of a marigold's fair crest.
'Tis old faithful *Magdalene*
with her tears and cloak as ever
watching o'er them both together.
    And my sight is not so bad
that it fails to see my own
Hyacinth, my darling lad,
midst the hyacinths has grown.
Where could such a lad be found,
slim and full of pious power,
Where so marvellous a flower
anywhere in rich Dutch ground?

Oh, and I see in this fine
calyx, amethyst in gleam,
Joseph's gentle, soulful mien,
as he did recite his dream.
And when all the dream was over,
this fantast his head would droop,
turn pale, and his gaze would lower
like the flowers when almost spent
of the hyacinth will stoop
once they've given off their scent.
    Fair convolvulus, as fine
as a seraph's breath divine,
caught by cherub, glad and proud,
in a flower's most fine-meshed net
in a harebell's linen shroud,
You are my *Elisabeth*,
who my Hyacinth would hear
with the most discerning ear
with your eyes so large and blue
blind with faith because so true.
    Would I then my best child know,
have a father's heart in vain,
had I not *Narcissa's* pain
read in this narcissus' glow?
if I no more understood
why she seems to lack all blood
from that glaring purple glimmer
from that image's bright shimmer
on that pledge ring broken only
by grim death, as dead one lonely,
which on her fair cheeks did play,

from the scalding drop so near
I in fright saw on a cheek
flare up and then disappear?
    Woe, its livid carmine streak,
Scar left by pain's vicious bite,
Judas kiss of death, foul blight,
still adorns her lovely cheek!
There is not so white a star,
pearl pale in its mortal coil
(lily risen from the soil
could quite probably be her)
Glow profound and coral's fire,
sun-drenched ruby cannot seem
in its heat to match this gleam.
    Woe, if after marks so dire,
which each glance enhances farther,
if I now with mind most fell,
will of an unnatural father,
with imagined look which slew
every trace of joy as well,
could distinguish twixt the two,
twixt this Whitsun daffodil
and Narcissa dying here!
    Oh, what boundless jubilation
for this hour saved quite entire!
Moment sweet, the mere duration
of an arrow you require,
of the blinking of sun's eye,
all the poison to extract
'gainst all bitterness react
of so many days' complaint,
of the waking pangs and sighs

of so many nights when faint
with great pain and mournful cry.
Do I live still? Is this eye,
ancient now, for its salvation
worthy of a revelation
so complete ere with its breath
it is polished clear by Death?
Look, now everyone is there!
Every rose among its roses,
look, there is the bridal pair
Katharina and *Johan!*
Love's divine apotheosis,
Katharina and *Johan!*
In each other's gaze full sated,
In shared images created,
they exchange their each heart's beat
mingling tears each other meet
in a lasting fond embrace,
they exchange their eyes' own light,
in each other beams ignite,
lips exchange the highest bliss,
lofty soundless oaths repeat
in each everlasting kiss.

  Blessed is the wedding hour,
flame-devoured yet here once more?
Teardrops mild of heav'nly grace
turned ash fertile and made new,
and the strength of my tears' dew
quickened the restoring pace,
fervent moans of my distress,
and my prayer's warming breath —
both my roses caused to push

upwards from the single bush:
Katharina and *Johan*,
both these bowed-down, sweetly scented,
in each other so contented
morning-fresh and morning-red
roses whispering a-bed –
Katharina and *Johan*.
    Up from these deep roses stream –
as from depths of magic bowls –
their fair features like a dream:
joyful sight that me consoles.
Since for them the wedding hour,
that which flames did once devour,
now once more its bliss imparts,
reuniting heart to heart,
Katharina to *Johan*.
I by heav'nly wonder can,
ancient pastor, now repeat
and their wedding day complete,
broken off on that dire day,
and my wedding speech now end
that the Walloon might so dread
cruelly forced me to suspend
ere the blessing could be said.
    Freely now, with laid on hands
May God bless these wedding bands,
May you gain the heavn'ly bliss,
Bride and bridegroom, that is His:
Lord, bless and maintain this pair
of bridal roses in Thy care!
Lord, lift up Thy countenance

over charm that makes its vows!
Lord, Thy glory of Thy face
lift o'er piety's bridal flowers
Lord, may Thy peace ever grace
this true⁄loving innocence!
  Oh, sweet instant of delight,
happy birth⁄time hour of bliss!
you with joy are far too weighted
to fly fleetingly astray
as the other down⁄grey, faded,
tintless hours of pale sunlight ,
breath of fate that's blown away
off across life's desert plain; —
you of instants are the jewel
that's been sent one time before
and is heaven⁄sent again,
not so treacherous and light
as the others, all so fleeting;
and, joy⁄laden, may you fuel
my old heart with speech once more,
till it gains its thought aright,
till tired it just for once may grow
of its purposeless loud beating,
till it just for once is sated
with the tears that joy's created,
while my ancient lips rejoice,
while my old eyes brightly glow,
while my words with falt'ring voice
(beauteous though as an unknown
language from high heaven's throne)
stumble as my tongue they find,

as if I had lost my mind.
  Oh it is as if my heart
drowned in silent, sultry rain,
as if the knot of my pain,
the dripping stone of my woe,
my sorrow-crystal of mind
resolved into benediction,
out into these tears must roll
covering the whole wide world,
swathing all its mountain peaks
in a cloud of generation,
with its sultry darkness' pressing
down must impregnate with blessing,
impregnate its depths anew
to a joyous, guiltless making.
  Oh where is there ample tongue
that could all my joy express,
ample vault within my breast,
ample air, or space, or sounds,
tender, quivering and high
that in tones could e'er inspire
my great joy that thus abounds?
ample mirrors in my eye
to reflect and catch it all?
ample senses to perceive it?
ample memory to hold it?
ample thoughts to take it in
ample nerve-strings fit and strong
to bear happiness for long?
ample heart to amply share
tenderness with all my treasures;
with Margretha, with the pair

of young ones smiling at her side,
with Narcissa who is ailing,
Hyacinth with dreaming air,
Strong in faith Elisabeth,
wonder-eager with each breath,
with my pride, my Katharine,
with the precious pledges heaven
has entrusted in my power,
growing once more in those flowers,
those there, all my family?

      Woe, unnatural father's heart
Made of dull, moss-covered stone!
I have yet forgotten one
of my selfsame flesh and bone:
poor young Klara's mortal anguish,
its pale image seems to be
in this white rose, for 'tis she,
'tis she herself. See the blush
struggles on her cheek as ever
in what is a dying flush,
one that pain with paleness tempers,
with the dark-white dying embers
of a passion that's burned down,
Chalk-dust of the ruined heaps
That beneath her air of mildness
crushed within her heart she keeps —
peace and innocence now lost!

      Oh my child, observe your father!
Rose so white that once was Klara!
He no longer would have chided
your sick love that was misguided,
He no gaze would now impress,

Crushing your crushed wretchedness,
He would have no passing glance
that would sear what went askance;
He has but a father's heart,
blessings that he would employ,
and a pain to match your pain
and a teardrop for the wound,
tears of sweet and fragrant joy;
for you too I have refound:
Now unbroken is my chain.
    Every one of you is present
So full of life and so true
that I cannot misconstrue
truth's vision with its appearance.
For within my soul it's sworn,
And my eyes confirm it too,
since I know you all too well:
Flowers you'd not only be
within my imagination,
you, my children and my wife,
for they're *you* assuredly,
yes, are you in soul and life,
you in features true to kind,
all distinctiveness of mind,
every nature's innate air,
smiles that can imprint in faces
fine as butterflies their traces
ere they quickly disappear.
    And I heard you softly speak,
if my senses did not sleep,
if death's grave-moss were not here

in the crevice of my ear.
But what senses does one need?
Eye will see if ear won't heed,
All is once again in flower,
All is now as once it was: —
Covered by a heav'nly dew,
Earth returns it all anew,
all as on that wedding day
when my happiness unfurled
every petal of its heart,
spreading out its crown's bright rays
farther than the sky condones,
when its full-grown flowering
up towards the clouds was towering
higher than heavenly ones will own,
at that moment it then burst
at the Almighty's high command
and flaming to the ground was hurled,
extinguished with a flame's swift thirst.

     Therefore — oh, is it that moment,
once again with life endued,
from time's chalice now returned,
when my pure, ecstatic joy
in frightful horrors was interred,
which in this way is renewed?
Therefore there are many traces
of flames, and clouds tinged with red,
full of demons' baleful gazes,
roaring with a hellish glee.

     They gleam again. Oh, woe is me!
Save me! Oh, all is now saved,

since the moment has now passed
when the tower came crashing down,
bored itself into the ground.
    Therefore now this tulip flower
(a real 'Admiral Enkhuizen')
that conceals its flaming depths
full of spots of whitish embers,
is not, only signifies
the house, once ablaze entire,
and the poppy there that soars
proudly and with flames adorned
o'er the flowerbed is the spire
when it toppled and fell down.
    And this bulb, a crimson red,
('Admiral van Liefkenshoek') —
like a night that's set alight,
like a fire that's painted night,
Living death, a life that's dead,
fiery⁄cold and powerful⁄paltry,
like a net⁄veiled giant's might,
spellbound demon mind beguiled —
this shall represent that swarthy,
enigmatic, pious, wild,
harsh yet gentle Spaniard who
when the terror greatest grew
dared to face the troops as though
he commanded hell below:
He with judgment on his brow
half the written then erased
in a stroke of clemency,
He with passion's fires ablaze
seething in pain's waters deep,

sated by his smile of anguish,
poisonous yet honey-sweet.
    And beside him see the monster,
see his comrade wild and bold,
see the soldier madly raging
in a double, gold-embroidered,
tiger-eyed large marigold –
He who had his dire intention
curbed by death's lone intervention!
    At this harmless mighty blazing,
at this flame that does not shriek,
at these terrors that can't daze,
at this flower-demon's traits,
I with features calm and bleak
and unblinking eye am gazing.
Down into the tulip's mine,
down into this copper hive,
full of wildly scattered sparks,
I dare stare with head unswimming;
with an eye that sees undimming
I now plumb the cauldron's depths
Dare to trace the fire-flower's flight
high into the sky's blue light,
dare exchange looks brave and grim,
glances eagle-bold, with him,
with that pious angelic killer,
with the Spaniard's soul that gleams
(to which fate God has condemned
him – a fate that should be chiller)
out of this bulb's growing stem
in the calyx deep that bleeds
with the black blood of disease.

Yes, this sight is dear to me,
whose significance is guessed
by a mind not greatly pressed:
Home on fire is in the tulip;
Tower on fire (like braided lightning
flash that from the depths streaks high)
in the poppy's scarlet eye;
Church roof with its length entire
in its flower's expansive fire;
And the Spaniard's wild distress
(as he stood there at the door –
bloody, frightful, though maybe
to save those present there from
either dreadful death by fire
or his comrades breaking in)
in the secretive, fold‑back,
warrior‑red and friar‑black
of that tulip's calyx‑bay
in which night and flame both play.
    Oh, these sights are dear to me,
Oh, I see with loving eye
the flower that flashes luridly,
with a colour burning high.
These flowers' lovely silent dread
only memory has fed,
my eyes they fill with delight,
my lips' dead smile they excite.
For they also do belong
to that selfsame hour of fate
when my faith was truly great,
to that selfsame hour of fate
when my bliss was truly strong,

when my soul was heaven nigh,
farthest from all mortal thought,
lightest under dread's great load.
At that moment, without doubt,
I did love my dear ones most,
just when death us all sought out
just when dread us interwove
and our lips the Lord were praising,
none of us dissent was raising.
     Oh, how can I have deserved
this your marvel, mighty Lord?
Should – oh, I am quite unnerved!
This poor worm would speak at fault! –
Should not you, yes, you yourself,
You, the holiest and greatest,
farther from first angel's courses
than from highest heaven's vault
deepest of the ocean's sources . . .
You, whom no name can depict,
You, to whom worlds are as flowers,
Grass that's by abysses borne,
Though but one of angel order
And midst spirits raised on high
That o'er all the earth hold sway,
should not you, in mercy strong,
done this miracle today,
this mere worm to satisfy,
make resemble his great lord,
when he centuries ahead,
lights extinguished stars once more
in the spaces long since dead,
     – Oh, then I would ask you, Lord,

that this angel you will bless
who's been good as you are good,
powerful with a kindliness
powerful in what most affords,
powerful in resembling God
loving – oh, as you're most loving!
Then I ask – Quiet! . . .

A tall, stately man, with a gold chain with the
Prince of Orange's portrait on his magnificent
black velvet doublet, with a diamond clasp on his
beret, a purse through which the gold glittered and
a dagger at his side, followed by a boy with a vase
full of flowers, steps over the heaps of rubble
between the elderberry bushes that surrounded old
Adrian's spot. He brushes them aside. —

JAN VAN HUYSUM,
THE FLOWER PAINTER

'Careful now, nameless one,' the stranger says, 'the flowers on these ruins are more magnifi-cent than those of the gardens. They have sucked their colour out of blood and calcified bones, and the flames have primed the soil.'

The old man takes fright. Even so, he does not get up from Margarethe's grass seat. For his only visitors were normally the storks that had returned from one of the remaining merlons – or the head of a curious innocent lizard among the stones, the shepherd's lad from the nearest village, some gypsy or an equally hurried traveller.

'Aha!' the stranger exclaims. 'Dear God! When did my eye ever see such flowers? These you have let grow for me, for me alone. Throw away, lad, these miserable water sprouts that you are carrying! These will become my masterpiece, as — with heaven's blessing — they have become the earth's.'

Adrian: 'You are right, stranger. They are so with heaven's blessing.'

'Woe that madness, woe to me
poor wretch, blinder than the blind
should God's wonder I dispute!'

The stranger: 'You must let me have them, old man.'
'No, no, no!'
'You must do so. I will pay for them.'
'That you cannot. Believe me, you cannot.'
'No, is that what you think!' And he throws his gold purse to Adrian.
'Not with your eyes, nor with your heart's blood.'
The face of the stranger turned scarlet. His eyes sparkled. 'I have told you, old man, that I must have them. There is the Prince of Orange and his gift!' And he hurls his gold chain and the diamond clasp at Adrian's feet. 'Are you satisfied now?'
'Your diamonds cannot make up for even one of the dewdrops on my flowers. Your eyes are

more intimidating than your speech. For God's
mercy's sake – what do you want?'

The stranger has drawn his dagger. 'Not
your life, but the flowers.'

'Yes, they are life! Madman, do not touch
them! I swear by my salvation and yours that they
are life, they are life!'

'Precisely so. This very moment I must have
them – in a moment's time they are not as they are
now.'

He is already kneeling down by the flowers.
The old man leaps up, his features petrified. The
stranger has already laid his steel against the stem of
the rose. He cuts. At the same instant, the lad lets
out a scream, and collapses, his hand on his heart.

'Benjamin, Benjamin, my child!' the old
man squeals, sinking back with death on his
visage.

The stranger wrestles the vase from the lad's
hand.

'What's the matter with you, lad? Nameless,
Nameless, my lad, did you feel ill at the strong
scent of these flowers? Or has a snake bitten you?'

The stem with the rose-flower is cut, and the
lad is dead.

> 'What is this? Ha, there's fresh blood
> on the cut stem with its bud,
> blood as in a wound that's open,
> and a drop too on my weapon.
> Now though all has disappeared;

now the pain, but not my fear
midst the joy at such a catch,
luckily has been dispatched.
Horror! was the life-cord then
Of my lifeless darling linked
directly to this flower? And
did his genius dwell therein?
Could he life with it have shared?
Doubly, with a force that's new,
it would seem to be inspired
in its sap of crimson hue.
Its bud, no more in sleep immersed,
seems to be alert in spirit
and its lip, should it but will it,
capable of speaking verse.
I must therefore hasten on,
End what was begun in sin;
I must hasten on ere you,
Rose Spirit, should change your view,
ere you choose to leave for sure
kindred petals evermore.'

The stranger encompasses the flowers with
trembling hands.
  'There is horror . . . in this, but I must
continue, while this gardener, who is insane in his
avarice and hides his mysteries in this remote
corner, cannot disturb me.'
  He looks at the old man, who has fainted,
and pauses yet a while.
  'Ha, who has ever refused Jan van Huysum,
the flower painter, a bouquet?'

Within three seconds Adrian's flowers are
resplendent in the painter's vase.

There is no more violent, ruthless, self-loving
passion than that of the artist. It knows no bounds,
rights or sins. It grasps for the object of its desire
with gigantic arms, for it believes it has the heart of
a god.

When, with enthusiastic gaze, he lifted up
the full, resplendent vase, the old man came to his
senses.

'Oh my God! My God! they have been
killed,' he groans with his hands before his eyes.

'In order to live for ever,' the proud painter
replies, lifting the vase on high.

'Take care of the lad. He was my adopted
son and possibly your child.'

'Yes, yes, he was . . . my Benjamin; and you
have murdered him, murdered them all, his
siblings, his mother and his father, who curse you
with the most terrible of all curses, with the curse
of your own child to madness of grief over your
own child. Yes, if God gives but a thousandth
measure for measure – you will beg in vain for
God's and your own child's mercy and that your
steely heart may break, that it may die like me.'

And the old man had dragged himself over
to the lad's dead body. 'Devil!' he moaned, 'you do
not know what you have done.' He sighed once
again and then no more.

'But I know what I will do, and what I can do,' the painter shouted, gazing yet more intently at the magnificent bouquet. But when he saw the old man's glazed eyes and his venerable hair over the pale, deathly features of the lad, a shiver passed through his large, nervous body; but he continued to mutter as he stole away with a fearful look, 'yes, I know what I will do. Who has ever refused Jan van Huysum a bouquet?'

Jan van Huysum painted Adrian's flowers. No more wonderful masterpiece ever flowed from his brush. Pangs of conscience – or perhaps rather an overwrought feeling of fear and presentiment – drove his genius to its highest pitch. He worked with the beating heart and hurried hand of the young medical novice who, at the hour of midnight, is dissecting a stolen corpse. At times, he thought he saw the faces of ghosts in the flowers, and Adrian's curse almost seemed to be fulfilled. From the instant he placed the vase in front of him and stretched out his canvas, he began to shut himself in when at work; he started to shun human society and became melancholic – but more marvellous in his works than ever before.

These characteristics were regarded as traits of an originality that belonged to his genius, and more people than one would have expected were sensible enough to think that unless Jan van Huysum were so bizarre, he would not be able to paint such wonderful flower pieces either, or be the man he was.

But people shook their heads and shrugged their shoulders and gave each other knowing looks when the great master buried the flowers with the utmost care in consecrated ground when they had withered – and said a prayer over them.

His godless son stood beside him and mocked and laughed at his father. It was one of the charaćteristics of his wickedness that allowed Adrian's curse to be fulfilled. For God hears the dying man; and the feeling of having committed a crime and the suspicion of having severed some of nature's secret strings that bound that old man's heart to life prepared his dark, receptive disposition for the fate that aćtually struck down the master: madness – as it was said, at the wickedness of his child.

There were also other causes. Two separate pains seized his heart at one and the same time when he quietly mumbled to himself: 'Benjamin! Benjamin!' This was in the heaviest hours. He then sought relief in the minute painting of the rosebud.

He worked constantly at his flower piece. It could never be perfeć enough. He seemed to recall a further beauty every time he lowered his hand and stroked his brow, as if he wanted to stroke away everything down to the bone. He could never bring himself to give the painting his mark of immortality, assuredly unnecessary except for duller eyes in the case of de Heem's, the flower poet, the brilliant creator of the 'Flower Altar', the man who relates to van Huysum as Pereira to

Velazquez and Alonzo de Tobar to Murillo. For every time he seized his brush to write his signature, there appeared some further inimitable suggestion of flies, snails and a bird's nest as well as a couple of flowers without that secret meaning, as things by means of which he sought to obscure from himself the meaning of the main group of flowers and to disappoint himself with the idea that he had simply painted nature as it is.

Finally, in a lighter moment – as the flowers seemed to bend towards him, the rose to open its lip and to pray – he again placed the tip of his brush to the canvas to make the signature: 'Jan van Huysum fecit'.

It is at the spot where the flowers were buried that he lifts up the painting in the afforded light. He smiles. Jan van Huysum's soul admits to itself in this moment that it is completed.

Then a drop falls on to it out of the clear sky. It bursts over the flowers. A marvel! The droplets remain where they fall, clinging there for ever, more firmly than the diamond in its rock, on Katharina's rose and on the other flowers.

'Old man! you are reconciled,' the master exultantly exclaims. 'It was your tear.' And he completes the signature, and from that instant calmness was restored in his heart.

No one know what spirits there are above him. But sometimes their presence is felt by more sensitive souls, and it is as if tears fall into our hearts.

Yes, assuredly it was old Adrian's tear that fell from the clear air. It is the tears of Adrian's reconciliation and admiration, as they still sit in the miraculously wonderful drops on Jan van Huysum's flower piece.

The years pass. The sea does not toss its prey more strangely than time the paintings of old masters, for people are eager for the divine to the same extent as this is perceptible. Therefore, paint⁄ings where this is the case swiftly pass from hand to hand down through the centuries, whereas a poem would die of bookshelf dust, or something even more ignominious, if the press did not save it by making it as common as the cobblestones.

Even so, this poem, too, will die before Jan van Huysum's flower piece lives through another year of its immortality.

The years pass. There was an exhibition at the Louvre of Napoleon's art trophies. Master⁄pieces from Spain, Italy and the Netherlands the great eagle had brought home with him to his nest under the tall colonnade. Among them were also 'Saint Katharina's Betrothal' by Alonzo de Tobar, Velazquez's 'Family' and another 'Family' by Alonzo de Tobar, as well as the great Jan van Huysum's 'Flower Piece'. The museum was full of viewers.

But the viewers were less concerned with admiring the masterpieces than mocking a young man who claimed there was a similarity which he felt more than he saw or was able to explain between one of the roses in Jan van Huysum's Flower Piece and Alonzo de Tobar's Katharina – indeed, between every one of the flowers and the individuals in his 'Family' after Velazquez. They laughed at him as the passers-by had done at old Adrian.

A tall, serious man dressed in black approaches the fantasist. The public draw aside respectfully. 'Follow me!' he say kindly, 'You are a painter.'

It was the master David who led Gros – the painter of 'Amor and Psyche' as his disciple to his studio.

Since David was not harsher, I too – without fearing the laughter of the public, which scarcely knows that, in accordance with the afore-mentioned irregularity of the circulation of master-pieces, it possesses in its midst Jan van Huysum's Flower Piece – dare say openly that it seems to me as if there is a mysterious similarity between that Amor and Psyche and the two roses in Jan van Huysum's Flower Piece.

– Ah, sweet rosebud, what tale have you told me about Jan van Huysum's Flower Piece while I was absorbed in contemplating it?

'But for certain now I know
how such flowers came to be.'

BIOGRAPHICAL NOTE

'In Norway, all evaluation of his poetic stature tends to
be coloured by his importance as a national symbol.'
R. G. Popperwell, *The Penguin Companion
to Literature*, 1969

His towering œuvre comprises visionary poems,
satirical farces, national anthems, sea shanties,
didactic poems for children, prose pieces, letters
and articles as well as the occasional treatise. The
style is high-flown, Romantic-Baroque and
extremely rich in images, especially in the early
poetry. A change of tempo seems to occur, one that
seems to coincide with his marriage in 1838 to the
young Amalie Sofie Bækkevold, a girl of humble
extraction. She has inspired some of the most
beautiful love poetry in Norwegian literature. And
on his death-bed – the year-long sickbed – he
wrote his most serene verses about his own illness
and impending death. Henrik Wergeland died
aged 37. And left behind him writing that fills 23
volumes.

In Protestant Norway, Wergeland has been idolised as the national patron saint that the Reformation sought to cheat us of. We can relate to him as a person – his writing is really too difficult for us. Here, the syllabus shrinks to a few appetisers that sixth-form pupils have to labour to understand, most of them without seeing the point of it all. Many leave school hating Wergeland. And yet there are more than 22¾ volumes that remain unread by most people. We are talking about the greatest and strangest poet Norway has produced.

His last words on his death-bed are said to have been a necessary clarification: 'I was a poet. Simply a poet.' Despite this, he has survived as much else besides. And he also did a lot of other things than write poetry.

For a long time after his death, he was especially used for political ends. And as such – posthumously – he played an important role in Norwegian history. His many changing or paradoxical points of view enabled people from the political Right and Left to parade his image like a banner. That the Left eventually gained monopoly of the banner was of crucial importance for the Norwegian struggle for independence. As late as during the Second World War, when Norway was an occupied country, Wergeland was brought forward as the great national bard. Since then, he has very frequently been mentioned in connection with the nation's self-celebration each year on

Constitution Day, 17 May. He has – somewhat unjustly – been given the honour of having established the celebration of this particular day.

Can it be this provincial idolising of the poet as a liberating hero in a farflung corner of Europe that has blinded the rest of the world to his genius? Can the world have thought: 'This will have to stay the Norwegians' national poet'? We have our Shakespeare, our Goethe, our Pushkin and Hugo – and, in spite of everything, they write in languages people can understand. Wergeland belongs in their company but, as he himself said, he was doomed to write for 'but a small, friendly flock'. It can be claimed as part of the explanation that Wergeland's poetry lies close to the pain threshold for untranslatability. His poetic language is so idiosyncratic that he does not have any direct successors in Norwegian literature either.

Henrik Arnold Wergeland, born in 1808 as the eldest son of a vicar (and 'philosopher', in the Enlightenment sense of the term), grew up in Eidsvoll, a small town north of the capital that has a key position in recent Norwegian history – it was here that the new, liberal constitution was drawn up and approved by an improvised constituent assembly in 1814. The poet's father had played an active role in that assembly.

The Wergeland family belonged to an upper class in a poor country. The poet's younger sister,

Camilla, became Norway's first female novelist. It is part of the story that she fell helplessly in love with her brother's antipole and enemy, the poet Welhaven, and later married another notorious enemy, the lawyer Collett. In the *Flower Piece*, Adrian's eldest daughter Klara – 'with a tragic passion for an enemy soldier' – may be a reminder of this difficult relationship.

His upbringing was liberal, strongly influenced by Nicolai Wergeland's enthusiasm for Rousseau, with a freedom to explore nature, free access to the neighbouring farms, uncensored access to his father's book collection and with the widely read father as one of the private tutors. At the early age of eleven, the boy was sent to school in Christiania (now Oslo), and only two years later he moved into lodgings and began to take part in the free, dissolute life of a student in the small capital. He was intellectually precocious, always curious and basically naïve. He read theology, like his father.

After 400 years of Danish hegemony, Norway was from 1814 onwards in a union with Sweden. The king of Sweden and Norway (from 1818) was the former French marshal Bernadotte, with the royal title King Karl Johan. The written language, officialdom and high culture were all strongly affected by the Danish era. Most of the officials were proDanish. Nicolai Wergeland was one of the exceptions – he had been in favour of union with Sweden and considered himself a friend of the king. His son, the republican, firebrand and agitator, also acquired a close, complex relation to Karl Johan. The king, for his part, found it difficult to deal with an admirer who was basically against the monarchy. It all ended with Wergeland being awarded an annual gratuity for his work in the cause of popular education – sneeringly referred to by opponents as a 'court pension'. Today, we would call it a government scholarship.

Wergeland had a big heart and a big ego – he was impulsive, obstinate and self-willed. He often acted unwisely. Norwegian intellectual life was also so small and small-minded that opponents immediately became bitter enemies. The intellectual struggle and the political struggle became personal and a considerable strain. In addition, Wergeland got embroiled in a series of ruinous lawsuits that took up a great deal of his time and energy. For all his greatness, he was a cantankerous individual.

Nor was his lifestyle irreproachable. That he never got a benefice was not due to his undogmatic interpretation of Holy Scripture, but to his disorderly conduct. He tried to change course by studying medicine, but never completed his studies or became a doctor. From 1840 onwards – thanks to a royal favour – he was given the post of keeper of public records, with the title of Assistant Secretary. In addition, he was allowed to keep his royal gratuity.

During his final years, he became increasingly isolated, excluded from society and refused access to the columns of the newspapers. Old friends turned their backs on him, old enemies hardened towards him even further. After the final, most serious lawsuit, he was practically bankrupt. At the same time, he fell seriously ill. His illness mainly affected his lungs, his breathing – whether pneumonia, lung cancer or tuberculosis, the diag⁄nosis is uncertain. It took fourteen months from his first attack until he died during the night of 12 July 1845, aged just 37. Many of his loveliest, most poignant poems were written on his death⁄bed. Thousands of people – a considerable number in such a small capital as Christiania – accompanied him to his grave. Most of those in the street were just average citizens, common people, the working class; only a handful were from his own station in life.

Wergeland believed in the individual's potential for self⁄improvement and in the forward movement of humanity. Freedom and enlighten⁄ment were what was needed. His work for popular education was motivated by this optimism. He wrote appeals for freedom of the press, religious freedom and freedom from tyrants. He published his own magazines, fought for the right of the poor to have an education, urged people to treat animals humanely and for years maintained a campaign to allow Jews to enter the country. The memorial on his grave was raised by 'grateful Jews outside the borders of the realm'.

TOM LOTHERINGTON, 2008